A Gift For

_____

From

_____

/

STRENGTH *for the* SOUL *from* OUR DAILY BREAD

Prayer

Discovery House Publishers

Books, music, and videos that feed the soul with the Word of God

Box 3566 Grand Rapids, MI 49501

Discovery House Publishers is affiliated with RBC Ministries,
Grand Rapids, Michigan.

Discovery House books are distributed to the trade exclusively by
Barbour Publishing, Inc., Uhrichsville, Ohio.

Interior design by Sherri L. Hoffman

Printed in Italy
06 07 08 09 / L.E.G.O. / 10 9 8 7 6 5 4 3 2 1

Introduction

Since April 1956, millions of readers around the world have found daily inspiration, help, comfort, and biblical truth from the pages of *Our Daily Bread*. Now you can find helpful insights on prayer from one of the most beloved devotionals, compiled into one convenient volume.

We hope that this book will be of help to you and those you know. May it and the Word of God bring strength to your soul.

Other books in the Strength for the Soul
from *Our Daily Bread* series

Comfort
Hope
Grief
Peace
Trust

Weighing a Prayer

"This, then, is how you should pray:

'Our Father in heaven,
hallowed be your name,
your kingdom come,
your will be done
on earth as it is in heaven.
Give us today our daily bread.
Forgive us our debts,
as we also have forgiven our debtors.
And lead us not into temptation,
but deliver us from the evil one.'" —Matthew 6:9–13

*S*oon after World War II, a tired-looking woman entered a store and asked the owner for enough food to make a Christmas dinner for her children. When he inquired how much she could afford, she answered, "My husband was killed in the war. Truthfully, I have nothing to offer but a little prayer." The man was not very sentimental, for a grocery store cannot be run like a breadline. So he said, "Write your prayer on a paper." To his surprise she plucked a little folded note out of her pocket and handed it to him, saying, "I already did that."

As the grocer took the paper, an idea struck him. Without even reading the prayer, he put it on the weight side of his old-fashioned scales, saying, "We shall see how much food this is worth." To his surprise, the scale would not go down when he put a loaf of bread on the other side. To his even greater astonishment, it would not balance when he added many more items. Finally he blurted out, "Well, that's all the scales will hold anyway. Here's a bag. You'll have to put them in yourself. I'm busy." With a tearful "thank you," the lady went happily on her way.

The grocer later found that the mechanism of the scales was out of order, but as the years passed, he often wondered if that really was the answer to what had occurred. Why did the woman have the prayer already written to satisfy his unpremeditated demands? Why did she come at exactly the time the mechanism was broken? Frequently he looked at that slip of paper upon which the woman's prayer was written, for amazingly enough, it read, "Please, dear Lord, give us this day our daily bread!"

—HENRY BOSCH

7

"Send What Is Best"

The Spirit helps us in our weakness. We do not know what we ought to pray for, but the Spirit himself intercedes for us with groans that words cannot express. And he who searches our hearts knows the mind of the Spirit, because the Spirit intercedes for the saints in accordance with God's will.   —ROMANS 8:26–27

Two men planted olive trees in their fields. Afterward the one prayed, "Dear Lord, my trees need water. Please send rain." The showers came! He then petitioned, "They need sunshine," and God bathed them with sunlight! Later he cried, "Father, my trees need something to make them hardy. Please send a frost tonight." It came but killed them all. Traveling over to the other man's grove, he found his olive trees flourishing. "How can this be?" he asked. The man replied, "When I prayed, I didn't ask for rain, sunshine, or frost, I just said, 'Lord, you made these trees. You know what they need. Just send what is best!'"

We know there is a place for definite prayer requests. As we recognize certain unmistakable needs, we should pray for specific answers in harmony with God's will. In such instances we rejoice in these promises: "This is the confidence we have in approaching God: that if we ask anything according to his will, he hears us. And if we know that he hears us—whatever we ask—we know that we have what we asked of him" (1 John 5:14–15). "The effective, fervent prayer of a righteous man avails much." (James 5:16 NKJV).

However, it is also true that there are times when, as the apostle Paul expressed it, "we do not know what we ought to pray for" (Romans 8:26). It is then that special comfort can be found in the assurance that "the Spirit himself intercedes for us with groans that words cannot express," and "the Spirit intercedes for the saints in accordance with God's will" (8:26–27).

When in doubt, we say with complete trust, "Lord, send what is best!"   —RICHARD DE HAAN

How God Answers Prayer

In Joppa there was a disciple named Tabitha (which, when translated, is Dorcas), who was always doing good and helping the poor. About that time she became sick and died, and her body was washed and placed in an upstairs room. Lydda was near Joppa; so when the disciples heard that Peter was in Lydda, they sent two men to him and urged him, "Please come at once!"

Peter went with them, and when he arrived he was taken upstairs to the room. All the widows stood around him, crying and showing him the robes and other clothing that Dorcas had made while she was still with them. Peter sent them all out of the room; then he got down on his knees and prayed. Turning toward the dead woman, he said, "Tabitha, get up." She opened her eyes, and seeing Peter she sat up. He took her by the hand and helped her to her feet. Then he called the believers and the widows and presented her to them alive. This became known all over Joppa, and many people believed in the Lord. —ACTS 9:36–42

The apostle Peter prayed and Dorcas was raised from death. Yet the apostle Paul asked the Lord three times to remove a physical affliction and He didn't do it. The Lord does not always give us what we would like to receive, and sometimes it seems as though He makes us wait a long time before He responds. I thought of this the other evening while attending a meeting where a number of people related striking answers to prayer. Some testified of physical healings that were nothing short of amazing, while others told of spiritual transformations in the lives of people for whom they had been praying. As these encouraging stories were being told, the faces of those present reflected the joy that came from their assurance of God's graciousness.

As I rejoiced with them, I couldn't help thinking of parents who had offered many earnest petitions but still saw their little ones die. I reflected upon the heartaches of mothers and fathers who have been interceding for wayward sons and daughters for many years, but have not as yet seen any evidence of an answer. No, prayer is not a magic wand by which we can always secure healing or success. The Lord hears and will respond to our prayers, but not necessarily in the way we expect.

When you kneel in your inner closet, acknowledge that God's will is best. If you are discouraged because He doesn't seem to answer, tell Him about it. Do not despair. He will either give you the desires of your heart, or He will undergird you with His supernatural power so that you will experience the truth of His wonderful promise, "My grace is sufficient for you" (2 Corinthians 12:9).　　　　—HERB VANDER LUGT

11

Praying in Public

"*And when you pray, do not be like the hypocrites, for they love to pray standing in the synagogues and on the street corners to be seen by men. I tell you the truth, they have received their reward in full. But when you pray, go into your room, close the door and pray to your Father, who is unseen. Then your Father, who sees what is done in secret, will reward you. And when you pray, do not keep on babbling like pagans, for they think they will be heard because of their many words. Do not be like them, for your Father knows what you need before you ask him.*"

—MATTHEW 6:5–8

When Jesus told people to pray in secret, He didn't mean that praying in public is wrong. What He condemned are insincere prayers made only to impress people. We may all sense that subtle temptation at times.

A group of delegates from a Christian conference stopped at a busy restaurant for lunch and were seated at several different tables around the room. Just before eating, one member announced in a loud voice, "Let's pray!" Chairs shifted and heads turned. Then followed a long-winded "blessing" that did more to cool the food than warm hearts. Finally, amid snickers and grumbling, came the welcome "Amen."

Contrast that story with another scene. A history teacher at a large state university was having lunch with his family in the school cafeteria. As they began their meal, their little three-year-old cried out, "O Daddy, we forgot to pray!" "Well, honey," said the man, "would you pray for us?" "Dear Jesus," she began, "thank You for our good food and all these nice people. Amen." From nearby tables came "amens" from professors and students alike who were touched by that child's simple and sincere prayer.

May all our public praying be like that.

—DENNIS DE HAAN

Invisible Support

The Amalekites came and attacked the Israelites at Rephidim. Moses said to Joshua, "Choose some of our men and go out to fight the Amalekites. Tomorrow I will stand on top of the hill with the staff of God in my hands."

So Joshua fought the Amalekites as Moses had ordered, and Moses, Aaron and Hur went to the top of the hill. As long as Moses held up his hands, the Israelites were winning, but whenever he lowered his hands, the Amalekites were winning. When Moses' hands grew tired, they took a stone and put it under him and he sat on it. Aaron and Hur held his hands up—one on one side, one on the other—so that his hands remained steady till sunset. So Joshua overcame the Amalekite army with the sword. . . .

Moses built an altar and called it The LORD is my Banner. He said, "For hands were lifted up to the throne of the LORD."

—EXODUS 17:8–13, 15–16

Prison guards couldn't understand how Irina Ratushinskaya could be so joyful. She was cold, sick, and hungry in a cruel Soviet prison camp. But Irina says she understands how: People were praying for her.

Irina is convinced that she and other prisoners experienced God's presence like "the sense of delicious warmth in a freezing land" because Christians all around the world were asking God to help them. After she was set free, Irina wrote a poem to express her gratitude to God and fellow believers. She included the words, "My dear ones, thank you all."

In our Scripture lesson we see that the Israelites prevailed over the superior Amalekite army when Moses lifted his staff toward heaven—a symbol of intercessory prayer. His praying on the hill, possibly unseen by the Israelites, gave them the invisible support they needed.

Sick, suffering, sorrowing people cannot see their fellow believers who are praying for them. But many people have told me they are amazed at the sense of God's presence in their affliction, and they know this to be the result of the prayers of their friends.

May we faithfully intercede for those who are struggling. Let's be a source of invisible support.

—HERB VANDER LUGT

A Stone or Bread

"Ask and it will be given to you; seek and you will find; knock and the door will be opened to you. For everyone who asks receives; he who seeks finds; and to him who knocks, the door will be opened.

"Which of you, if his son asks for bread, will give him a stone? Or if he asks for a fish, will give him a snake? If you, then, though you are evil, know how to give good gifts to your children, how much more will your Father in heaven give good gifts to those who ask him!"

—MATTHEW 7:7–11

No loving father would give a stone or a snake to his hungry son if he asked him for a piece of bread or a fish. Jesus used the absurdity of that analogy to underscore God's readiness to give good things to His disciples when they asked Him (Matthew 7). He wanted them to have complete confidence in the heavenly Father's provision for their spiritual needs.

Sometimes, however, it may seem as if the Lord has given us "stones" instead of "bread." But in His wisdom, He actually is working through our circumstances to give us something far better than what we requested. An unknown author expressed it this way:

> I asked for health that I might do greater things;
> I was given infirmity that I might do better things.
> I asked God for strength that I might achieve;
> I was made weak that I might learn to obey.
> I asked for riches that I might be happy;
> I was given poverty that I might be wise.
> I asked for power and the praise of men;
> I was given weakness to sense my need of God.
> I asked for all things that I might enjoy life;
> I was given life that I might enjoy all things.
> I got nothing I asked for but everything I hoped for;
> In spite of myself, my prayers were answered—
> I am among all men most richly blest.

Yes, God always gives us what's best for us.

—RICHARD DE HAAN

"We Just Have To Talk"

Now Moses used to take a tent and pitch it outside the camp some distance away, calling it the "tent of meeting." Anyone inquiring of the LORD would go to the tent of meeting outside the camp. And whenever Moses went out to the tent, all the people rose and stood at the entrances to their tents, watching Moses until he entered the tent.

As Moses went into the tent, the pillar of cloud would come down and stay at the entrance, while the LORD spoke with Moses. Whenever the people saw the pillar of cloud standing at the entrance to the tent, they all stood and worshiped, each at the entrance to his tent. The LORD would speak to Moses face to face, as a man speaks with his friend. —EXODUS 33:7–11

Lisa and Sheryl have been friends since grade school. Although their paths have taken them in different directions since those schoolgirl days in New Jersey, they have maintained their close friendship.

Sheryl is married, settled in the Midwest, and the mother of young children. Lisa is single and involved in mission work, most recently in Russia. "Every now and then we just have to talk," says Sheryl. So they pick up the phone to catch up on the news and share their hearts.

In our Bible reading today we learn that Moses and the Lord talked "as a man speaks with his friend" (Exodus 33:11). Moses enjoyed not merely an occasional phone call with the Lord, but frequent, direct conversation with Him that other Israelites could only observe from a distance. During those intimate talks, the Lord gave Moses instructions for leading the people.

Because of what Jesus Christ has done for us, and because the Holy Spirit now lives within all followers of Christ, we too can enjoy a special friendship and closeness with God. He speaks to us through His Word and by His Spirit, and we have the privilege of talking to Him in prayer.

If you are like me, as you go through your day you'll find yourself saying to God, "We just have to talk."

—DAVE EGNER

ACTS
of Prayer

One day Jesus was praying in a certain place. When he finished, one of his disciples said to him, "Lord, teach us to pray, just as John taught his disciples."

He said to them, "When you pray, say:

"'Father, hallowed be your name,
your kingdom come.
Give us each day our daily bread.
Forgive us our sins,
for we also forgive everyone who sins against us.
And lead us not into temptation.'" —LUKE 11:1–4

*W*hen my children come to me for advice, I consider it an honor to teach them what they need to know. For example, my daughter Julie had to write a poem for school not long ago. As I thought about the best way to assist her, I decided to compose a few lines to help her see how it's done.

Jesus used the example method when His disciples asked Him to teach them how to pray. Instead of going into a long dissertation on the subject, He said, "When you pray, say, . . ." and He gave them a pattern that also included prayer principles.

That prayer has at least four elements we can learn to use when we pray: Adoration, Confession, Temptation protection, and Supplication. Let's consider the ACTS of prayer.

Adoration: "Hallowed be your name." We need to give allegiance and respect to our great and awesome God.

Confession: "Forgive us our sins." God is "faithful and just and will forgive us" (1 John 1:9).

Temptation protection: "And lead us not into temptation." Ask for help to say no to sin.

Supplication: "Give us each day our daily bread." We should not be afraid to ask God for His provisions.

There's the example. It's up to us to follow it.

—DAVE BRANON

Put Your Fears To Rest

I sought the LORD, and he answered me;
*   he delivered me from all my fears.*
Those who look to him are radiant;
*   their faces are never covered with shame.*
This poor man called, and the LORD heard him;
*   he saved him out of all his troubles.*
The angel of the LORD encamps around those who fear him,
*   and he delivers them.*
Taste and see that the LORD is good;
*   blessed is the man who takes refuge in him.*

—PSALM 34:4–8

*I*t was the night before Steven would lose his adenoids and tonsils to a surgeon's scalpel. Being nine years old, he was fearful of what the next day would bring. The old "You get to have all the ice cream you can eat" line had worn itself out. Steven knew he was in for some tough days ahead.

Then the phone rang. It was our pastor, Jim Jeffery, calling Steven from an airport while on an out-of-town trip. When Steven got off the phone, he proudly announced, "Pastor Jeffery prayed with me on the phone!"

Later, after Steven had recovered from the surgery, he went to Pastor Jeffery to thank him for the phone call. He told him something he hadn't told us: "After you prayed with me on the phone, I wasn't scared anymore."

Prayer is a powerful tool whether we pray alone or with others. The psalmist cried out to the Lord and was delivered from his fears (Psalm 34:4). In Steven's case, prayer helped a young boy who feared an unknown tomorrow. In your case, it may help you understand God's mysterious ways when you lose a job, a relationship falters, a child goes wayward, or your faith seems small.

Share your concerns with others, and talk to the Father together. It's a great way to put your fears to rest.

—DAVE BRANON

Prayer Patrol

Be joyful in hope, patient in affliction, faithful in prayer.

—ROMANS 12:12

I thank God, whom I serve, as my forefathers did, with a clear conscience, as night and day I constantly remember you in my prayers. —2 TIMOTHY 1:3

I was headed out the door one morning when my wife Sue said, "Don't forget to pray for Julie. She has a big test today." It's not unusual for Sue to give me a reminder like that before I leave. "Don't worry," I replied, "I'll be on prayer patrol!"

In reality, we all need to be on prayer patrol all the time. When we are, we follow in the tradition of patrol members like Daniel, who prayed despite opposition (Daniel 6:10); the widow Anna, who prayed night and day (Luke 2:36–37); Paul, who prayed for his friends in Rome (Romans 1:9); and Cornelius, a God-fearing soldier who did double-duty by being in constant prayer (Acts 10:1–2).

God's Word contains our marching orders for being on prayer patrol. Some of them are:

- Pray without ceasing (1 Thessalonians 5:17).
- Continue steadfastly in prayer (Romans 12:12).
- Pray morning, noon, and night (Psalm 55:17).
- Pray always and do not get discouraged (Luke 18:1).

It's not difficult to find enough things to pray about. There are needs everywhere. The tough part is following through on our commitment to pray. Remind yourself throughout the day that you have a job to do. People are counting on you. You're on prayer patrol. —DAVE BRANON

Persistent Prayer

Then Jesus told his disciples a parable to show them that they should always pray and not give up. He said: "In a certain town there was a judge who neither feared God nor cared about men. And there was a widow in that town who kept coming to him with the plea, 'Grant me justice against my adversary.'

"For some time he refused. But finally he said to himself, 'Even though I don't fear God or care about men, yet because this widow keeps bothering me, I will see that she gets justice, so that she won't eventually wear me out with her coming!'"

And the Lord said, "Listen to what the unjust judge says. And will not God bring about justice for his chosen ones, who cry out to him day and night? Will he keep putting them off? I tell you, he will see that they get justice, and quickly. However, when the Son of Man comes, will he find faith on the earth?"

—LUKE 18:1–8

A friend of mine has been a woman of prayer for many years. She has received countless answers from God, but sometimes she is disheartened because certain prayers for loved ones remain unanswered. Yet she keeps on praying, encouraged by the parable in Luke 18, which features a widow who badgered a heartless judge for help and finally got it. Jesus ended His parable with a question: If an unrighteous and disrespectful judge finally answers a pestering widow's pleas for help, shall not God answer His own children who cry to Him day and night? The expected answer: "Of course He will!"

George Müller (1805–1898), pastor and orphanage director, was known for his faith and persistent prayer. Whenever he prayed for specific needs for his orphanage, God sent exactly what was required. Yet for more than forty years he also prayed for the conversion of a friend and his friend's son. When Müller died, these men were still unconverted. God answered those prayers, however, in His own time. The friend was converted while attending Müller's funeral, and the son a week later!

Do you have a special burden or request? Keep on praying! Trust your loving heavenly Father to answer according to His wisdom and timing. God honors persistent prayer!

—JOANIE YODER

Getting into the Habit

But I call to God,
    and the LORD saves me.
Evening, morning and noon
    I cry out in distress,
    and he hears my voice.
He ransoms me unharmed
    from the battle waged against me,
    even though many oppose me. . . .
Cast your cares on the Lord
    and he will sustain you;
    he will never let the righteous fall.

—PSALM: 55:16–18, 22

The family car is packed to the limit. The kids have their books, tapes, and games. The cartop carrier clearly signals to all observers that our family is taking a trip. But before we leave the driveway, we always stop and pray—asking God for safety and for family unity on our trip. It's a habit.

Prayer habits are helpful tools to remind us of our dependence on God. Perhaps you have some habits of your own. Before you eat, you pray. Maybe before the kids leave for school, you pray. Before they go to bed, you pray.

Developing prayer habits can be of tremendous help to those of us who want to develop a close relationship with the Lord but find that the busyness of the day squeezes out the time we had hoped to spend with Him. When we designate different activities of the day before or after which we always pray, we'll help to assure ourselves of regular communication with our Creator. That could become empty ritual, but it doesn't have to be—it can be a time of rich fellowship with our Lord.

David said that he prayed in the morning, noon, and evening (55:17). Daniel prayed three times a day (Daniel 6:10). Like them, we would be wise to develop prayer habits. They're great ways to make prayer an integral, constant part of our daily lives.   —DAVE BRANON

Keeping Track of Prayers

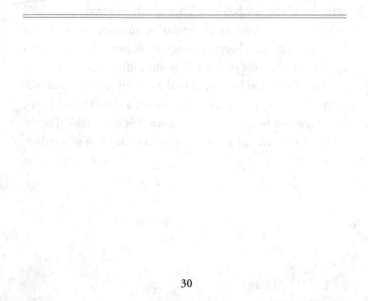

I write these things to you who believe in the name of the Son of God so that you may know that you have eternal life. This is the confidence we have in approaching God: that if we ask anything according to his will, he hears us. And if we know that he hears us—whatever we ask—we know that we have what we asked of him. —1 JOHN 5:13–15

*S*hortly before Margaret Koster died in 1997, I wrote an article about her, telling of her diligence in prayer. Despite her age, she set an example of faithfulness in prayer—continuing to spend hours each day speaking with the Lord she loved. Now she's reaping the rewards of that faithfulness.

But there's another story about Margaret that needs to be told—a story of how seriously she took her prayer-life. When she was younger, Margaret would pray each day for missionaries she knew about. She also kept a journal of her prayers, complete with answers.

One time when one of "her" missionaries was home from his overseas ministry, Margaret approached him, showed him her journal, and said, "I have recorded every prayer request you made as a missionary. And I have put down every answer that I know of. But I also have some prayers for which I don't know the answers. You need to sit down with me and tell me how God answered those prayers so I can write them down."

Now that's taking prayer seriously! We learn from Margaret not only the importance of prayer but also the reality of God's answers. Remember, "If we ask anything according to his will, he hears us" (1 John 5:14). —DAVE BRANON

You Can Always Pray

The night before Herod was to bring him to trial, Peter was sleeping between two soldiers, bound with two chains, and sentries stood guard at the entrance. Suddenly an angel of the Lord appeared and a light shone in the cell. He struck Peter on the side and woke him up. "Quick, get up!" he said, and the chains fell off Peter's wrists.

Then the angel said to him, "Put on your clothes and sandals." And Peter did so. "Wrap your cloak around you and follow me," the angel told him. Peter followed him out of the prison . . .

Then Peter came to himself and said, "Now I know without a doubt that the Lord sent his angel and rescued me from Herod's clutches and from everything the Jewish people were anticipating." When this had dawned on him, he went to the house of Mary the mother of John, also called Mark, where many people had gathered and were praying. Peter knocked at the outer entrance . . . and when they opened the door and saw him, they were astonished.   —ACTS 12:6-9, 11-13, 16

The young mother called out to the missionary, "Come quick! My baby is going to die." Gale Fields was in Irian Jaya helping her husband Phil translate the Bible into Orya, a tribal language. But they also provided medical help whenever possible. Gale looked at the malaria-stricken child and realized she didn't have the right medicine to help the infant.

"I'm sorry," she told the mother, "I don't have any medicine for babies this small." Gale paused, then said, "I could pray for her though."

"Yes, anything to help my baby," answered the mother.

Gale prayed for the baby and then went home feeling helpless. After a little while, she again heard the mother cry out, "Gale, come quick and see my baby!"

Expecting the worst, Gale went to the baby's side. This time, though, she noticed improvement. The dangerous fever was gone. Later, Gale would say, "No wonder the Orya Christians learned to pray. They know God answers."

The early Christians prayed for Peter to be released from prison and then were "astonished" when God answered them (Acts 12:16). We respond that way too, but we shouldn't be surprised when God answers our prayers. Remember, His power is great and His resources are endless. —DAVE BRANON

Who's Praying?

To Timothy, my dear son: Grace, mercy and peace from God the Father and Christ Jesus our Lord. I thank God, whom I serve, as my forefathers did, with a clear conscience, as night and day I constantly remember you in my prayers.

Recalling your tears, I long to see you, so that I may be filled with joy. I have been reminded of your sincere faith, which first lived in your grandmother Lois and in your mother Eunice and, I am persuaded, now lives in you also. For this reason I remind you to fan into flame the gift of God, which is in you through the laying on of my hands. For God did not give us a spirit of timidity, but a spirit of power, of love and of self-discipline.

— TIMOTHY 1:2–7

Jim Cymbala's daughter had been running from God for a long time. Chrissy had rebelled against her family, had left home, and was living as far from God as she could. But one night, this teenager awoke with the distinct feeling that someone was praying for her.

And someone was. The entire congregation of the church her father pastored was talking to God about her. During their weekly prayer meeting, a member had suggested they should all pray for Chrissy.

Two days later, she came home. The first question she had for her startled father was "Who was praying for me?" Then she begged forgiveness and recommitted her life to Christ.

In the apostle Paul's second letter to Timothy, he told the young first-century pastor that he was praying for him night and day (1:3). Timothy was facing some big challenges, so it must have been encouraging to know that Paul was praying specifically for him.

Are there some people you know who are in bondage to sin as Chrissy was, or who are facing a challenge as Timothy was? Are you willing to spend some concentrated time praying for them? Are you confident that God will answer?

Who's praying? We all should be.   —DAVE BRANON

My Life, My Plant

"But I am the LORD your God,
    who brought you out of Egypt.
You shall acknowledge no God but me,
    no Savior except me.
I cared for you in the desert,
    in the land of burning heat.
When I fed them, they were satisfied;
    when they were satisfied, they became proud;
    then they forgot me.
                    —HOSEA 13:4–6

Guests probably wonder why I keep a scraggly fern in my living room. I've gotten so used to its unsightliness that I seldom think to explain. The plant symbolizes a friendship that has become fragile, and I keep it in a prominent place as a reminder to pray for my friend, which I do whenever I water it. Its dried leaves make it obvious that I don't water it often enough, which also means that I don't pray often enough for my friend.

My fern is drying up because I don't water it until it wilts, and I carry that attitude along with me into my spiritual life. As long as my life is not in crisis, I figure that prayer can wait a while. But I'm wrong. When God's blessings make me think I don't need Him, I am more needy than ever.

The book of Hosea summarizes God's relationship with His chosen nation in words that parallel my own spiritual experience. God blesses, I grow; God satisfies, I take credit; God withholds His blessing, I realize my neediness; God reveals my sin, I repent; God forgives, I renew my devotion.

I've learned from my plant that I must pray even when I don't see the need. I need God just as much when I'm being blessed as when I am in crisis.   —JULIE ACKERMAN LINK

Our Prayer Partner

We know that the whole creation has been groaning as in the pains of childbirth right up to the present time. Not only so, but we ourselves, who have the firstfruits of the Spirit, groan inwardly as we wait eagerly for our adoption as sons, the redemption of our bodies. For in this hope we were saved. But hope that is seen is no hope at all. Who hopes for what he already has? But if we hope for what we do not yet have, we wait for it patiently.

In the same way, the Spirit helps us in our weakness. We do not know what we ought to pray for, but the Spirit himself intercedes for us with groans that words cannot express. And he who searches our hearts knows the mind of the Spirit, because the Spirit intercedes for the saints in accordance with God's will.

—ROMANS 8:22–27

My son Brian had been struggling for several hours to repair the plumbing in his bathroom. No matter what he tried, nothing seemed to work. His four-year-old son J. D. had been watching his dad, wanting to help but not knowing what to do. Brian was about to make one more try, but before doing so he looked up at J. D. and said, "Please pray."

The boy didn't know what to say, so he began with his usual nighttime requests: "Dear God, bless Dad, bless Mom, bless Sarah, bless Julia. Amen." Brian tried once more to fix the problem—and this time he succeeded.

Often we feel like J. D., not knowing what words to say. But we still come to God with our need because our confidence lies not in ourselves nor in our intercession, but in the Holy Spirit. He hears and knows our hearts, but He also hears and knows the heart of God the Father. George MacDonald wrote, "Father . . . look deep, yet deeper, in my heart, and there, beyond what I know, read Thou the prayer."

God's Spirit takes our inadequate prayers, breathes into them the Father's will, and turns them into meaningful requests (Romans 8:26). Although we may not get what we thought we wanted, we will receive God's best, for our Prayer Partner knows our deepest needs.   —DAVID ROPER

Something Far Better

You want something but don't get it. You kill and covet, but you cannot have what you want. You quarrel and fight. You do not have, because you do not ask God. When you ask, you do not receive, because you ask with wrong motives, that you may spend what you get on your pleasures. —JAMES 4:2–3

Now to him who is able to do immeasurably more than all we ask or imagine, according to his power that is at work within us, to him be glory in the church and in Christ Jesus throughout all generations, for ever and ever! Amen.

—EPHESIANS 3:20–21

A man who lived far out in the country bought his clothing from a mail-order catalog. At the bottom of the printed order form he noticed this statement: "If we do not have the article you ordered in stock, may we substitute?"

The first time that he wrote "yes," they sent him something that was worth double the price of the article he had requested. The company explained, "We are sorry we do not have the article in stock which you ordered. We are sending you something better at our expense."

After that, the man said he always printed out much more boldly the word "yes" at the bottom of the order blank. He knew he would not be disappointed by the substitution.

So too, when we pray to God, it is good to tell Him that we are quite willing to let Him take our weak prayers and answer them according to His will. Too often we pray and do not see our requests answered because we selfishly "ask with wrong motives" (James 4:3). Instead, we need to examine the motives of our hearts and trust Him to give us exactly what we need. We can be sure that when we do He will send us something far better, yes, "immeasurably more than all we ask or imagine" (Ephesians 3:20).

—HENRY BOSCH

Bite-Size Requests

In the morning, as they went along, they saw the fig tree withered from the roots. Peter remembered and said to Jesus, "Rabbi, look! The fig tree you cursed has withered!"

"Have faith in God," Jesus answered. "I tell you the truth, if anyone says to this mountain, 'Go, throw yourself into the sea,' and does not doubt in his heart but believes that what he says will happen, it will be done for him. Therefore I tell you, whatever you ask for in prayer, believe that you have received it, and it will be yours."

—MARK 11:20–24

*L*ots of things are easier to do when they're bite-size. If you have a major task to get done, for example, it helps to divide it into smaller units and tackle them one at a time. This is true whether you are redecorating the house, packing for a vacation, or directing a church project.

Rosalind Rinker suggests that the same is true of prayer. She found that when she made very general, all-inclusive requests of God, it seemed that nothing happened. But when she began making specific, bite-size requests, she saw results.

She recommends that we make our requests very specific, and ask for what we really believe is according to God's will. Rinker adds that as we see God's answers to relatively small requests, we will find that we are asking for bigger needs with a greater degree of faith.

Have you been praying general, world-encompassing prayers without seeing results? It's wiser to ask for something smaller and more specific and really believe that it will be answered. For example, rather than asking God to destroy all the pornography in the world, it would be better to pray that the convenience store on the corner would stop selling it. Then ask God what you can do to help bring that about.

Let's begin making bite-size requests!   —Dave Egner

Shut the Door!

"And when you pray, do not be like the hypocrites, for they love to pray standing in the synagogues and on the street corners to be seen by men. I tell you the truth, they have received their reward in full. But when you pray, go into your room, close the door and pray to your Father, who is unseen. Then your Father, who sees what is done in secret, will reward you. And when you pray, do not keep on babbling like pagans, for they think they will be heard because of their many words. Do not be like them, for your Father knows what you need before you ask him."

—MATTHEW 6:5–8

*Y*ears ago, a man who was visiting the United States wanted to make a telephone call. He entered a phone booth but found it to be different from those in his own country. It was beginning to get dark, so he had difficulty finding the number in the directory. He saw a light in the ceiling but didn't know how to turn it on.

As the man tried again to find the number, a passerby noticed his plight and said, "Sir, if you want to turn the light on, you have to shut the door." To the visitor's amazement, when he closed the door, the booth was filled with light. He soon located the number and completed the call.

In a similar way, when we draw aside to a quiet place to pray (Matthew 6:6), we must "shut the door" to block out our busy world. As we open our hearts to the Father, we receive the light of His wisdom. Our Lord often went to be alone with His heavenly Father for strength and guidance. Sometimes it was after a busy day of preaching and healing (Luke 5:12–16). At other times, it was before making a major decision (Luke 6:12–13).

We can have the confidence that "if we ask anything according to his will, he hears us" (1 John 5:14). But we must remember that to "turn the light on," we must first "shut the door" by getting alone with God. —RICHARD DE HAAN

A Powerful Lesson

For this reason, ever since I heard about your faith in the Lord Jesus and your love for all the saints, I have not stopped giving thanks for you, remembering you in my prayers. I keep asking that the God of our Lord Jesus Christ, the glorious Father, may give you the Spirit of wisdom and revelation, so that you may know him better.

I pray also that the eyes of your heart may be enlightened in order that you may know the hope to which he has called you, the riches of his glorious inheritance in the saints, and his incomparably great power for us who believe. That power is like the working of his mighty strength, which he exerted in Christ when he raised him from the dead and seated him at his right hand in the heavenly realms, far above all rule and authority, power and dominion, and every title that can be given, not only in the present age but also in the one to come. —EPHESIANS 1:15–21

In 1892, John Hyde boarded a ship in New York harbor and set out for India. His goal was to proclaim the gospel to people who had not heard about Jesus. During the next twenty years he earned the nickname "Praying Hyde" because he often spent hours and even days in prayer for the salvation of nonbelievers and the revival of Christ's followers.

On one occasion, Hyde was upset about the spiritual coldness of a pastor, so he began to pray, "O Father, you know how cold—" But it was as if a finger stopped his lips from uttering the man's name.

Hyde was horrified when he realized that he had judged the man harshly. He confessed his critical spirit and then determined not to focus on the shortcomings of others but to see them as individuals whom God loves. Hyde asked the Lord to show him things that were "of good report" (Philippians 4:8 NKJV) in the pastor's life, and he praised God for the man's virtues. Hyde learned later that during this exact time the pastor's spiritual life was revitalized.

Let's not be faultfinders—even in prayer. We can follow Paul's example of focusing on what God has done and what He can do in the lives of others (Ephesians 1:17–21). Instead of praying against people, let's pray for them.   —JOANIE YODER

The Listening Prayer

Hear, O Lord, and answer me,
*   for I am poor and needy.*
Guard my life, for I am devoted to you.
*   You are my God; save your servant*
*   who trusts in you . . .*
Teach me your way, O Lord,
*   and I will walk in your truth;*
give me an undivided heart,
*   that I may fear your name.*   —PSALM 86:1–2, 11

How do you feel when you talk with someone who isn't listening to you? It can happen with a friend who has his own plans for how a conversation should go. Or it can happen when the other person simply doesn't want to hear what you have to say.

Now think about this in regard to your prayer life. Could it be that the way we talk to God is a one-sided conversation dominated by us? Notice the observation of William Barclay in *The Plain Man's Book of Prayers*: "Prayer is not a way of making use of God; prayer is a way of offering ourselves to God in order that He should be able to make use of us. It may be that one of our great faults in prayer is that we talk too much and listen too little. When prayer is at its highest, we wait in silence for God's voice to us."

We might call this "the listening prayer," and it's a practice we need to develop. We need to find a way to get alone with God in quiet, to speak to Him in earnest, taking time to listen to the urgings of the Spirit and the instruction of His Word. We must say, "Teach me Your way, O LORD, and I will walk in Your truth" (Psalm 86:11).

Are we talking so much that we don't hear what God says? If so, we need to learn the art of the listening prayer.

—DAVE BRANON

Praying and Working

Jesus went through all the towns and villages, teaching in their synagogues, preaching the good news of the kingdom and healing every disease and sickness. When he saw the crowds, he had compassion on them, because they were harassed and helpless, like sheep without a shepherd. Then he said to his disciples, "The harvest is plentiful but the workers are few. Ask the Lord of the harvest, therefore, to send out workers into his harvest field."

—MATTHEW 9:35–38

While driving through a small town in Pennsylvania, I saw these words on a church sign: "Pray for a good harvest, but keep on hoeing." This made me think of Jesus' words in Matthew 9. Before telling His disciples to pray that laborers would be sent out, He reminded them that a good harvest was waiting but that the laborers were few (vv. 37–38).

We sometimes forget that God may want us to be part of the answer to our own prayers. We expect Him to do everything while we sit back and do nothing.

We ask Him to bless the work of our church but offer excuses when asked to serve. We plead for loved ones to be saved, yet never speak a word of testimony to them. We earnestly intercede for people with serious financial needs, but we won't dig deep into our own pockets even though we have the means to help them. We ask the Lord to comfort and encourage the shut-ins and lonely, but we never pay them a visit or send them a note of encouragement.

Yes, God wants us to bring our requests to Him. But many times He wants us to add feet to our prayers. Working often goes hand-in-hand with praying.   —RICHARD DE HAAN

Trust . . . and Prepare

When Jesus had called the Twelve together, he gave them power and authority to drive out all demons and to cure diseases, and he sent them out to preach the kingdom of God and to heal the sick. He told them: "Take nothing for the journey—no staff, no bag, no bread, no money, no extra tunic. Whatever house you enter, stay there until you leave that town. If people do not welcome you, shake the dust off your feet when you leave their town, as a testimony against them." So they set out and went from village to village, preaching the gospel and healing people everywhere . . .

Then Jesus asked them, "When I sent you without purse, bag or sandals, did you lack anything?"

"Nothing," they answered.

He said to them, "But now if you have a purse, take it, and also a bag; and if you don't have a sword, sell your cloak and buy one. It is written: 'And he was numbered with the transgressors'; and I tell you that this must be fulfilled in me. Yes, what is written about me is reaching its fulfillment."

—LUKE 9:1–6; 22:35–37

*I*n the early years after I began working with others in full-time Christian ministry, sometimes there was no money for our salaries. But looking back, I see that I have lacked nothing.

When Jesus sent out His disciples to preach, He told them to go without money, food, or extra clothes (Luke 9:3). Later, though, just before His arrest, Jesus told the disciples to bring along a moneybag and knapsack (Luke 22:36).

Was Jesus contradicting Himself? No. I believe He was teaching two parallel lessons. He wanted His disciples to learn to depend on Him, and He wanted them to prepare for the tough times ahead.

These two principles of Jesus—depending on Him as we serve Him, and doing what we can to be ready for future situations—are principles by which I seek to live and minister. I learned early in my ministry that we must be obedient to the Lord and trust Him to meet our daily needs. But I also believe He wants us to be wise and to do what we can to prepare for the future.

We tend to think we need to do one or the other. But the Lord wants us to trust . . . and prepare.   —ALBERT LEE

When Friends Fail You

After the LORD had said these things to Job, he said to Eliphaz the Temanite, "I am angry with you and your two friends, because you have not spoken of me what is right, as my servant Job has. So now take seven bulls and seven rams and go to my servant Job and sacrifice a burnt offering for yourselves. My servant Job will pray for you, and I will accept his prayer and not deal with you according to your folly. You have not spoken of me what is right, as my servant Job has." So Eliphaz the Temanite, Bildad the Shuhite and Zophar the Naamathite did what the LORD told them; and the LORD accepted Job's prayer.

After Job had prayed for his friends, the LORD made him prosperous again and gave him twice as much as he had before.

—JOB 42:7–10

With friends like his, Job didn't need enemies. His three would-be comforters failed miserably in their efforts to ease his pain. Instead of bringing sympathy, they delivered accusations that only compounded his anguish.

Yet Job was able to emerge triumphantly from his cave of pain and confusion. A significant step toward that victory was his willingness to pray for the very friends who had criticized and accused him. God honored his prayers, and Job had the delight of seeing his friends turn to God for forgiveness (Job 42:7–10).

Jesus also prayed for His friends (John 17:6–19), despite their frequent failings. With the agony of the cross approaching, Jesus prayed for Peter even though He knew Peter would deny Him within hours (Luke 22:31–34).

Jesus prayed for you and me too (John 17:20–26). His work of prayer, which began before His death and resurrection, continues to this day. Although we sometimes act more like His enemies than His friends, Jesus is in the Father's presence interceding for us (Romans 8:34; Hebrews 7:25).

Following Christ's example, we are to pray for our friends and acquaintances—even when they hurt us. Is there someone you can pray for today?　　　　　—HADDON ROBINSON

Nothing to Do
But Pray

The end of all things is near. Therefore be clear minded and self-controlled so that you can pray. Above all, love each other deeply, because love covers over a multitude of sins. Offer hospitality to one another without grumbling. Each one should use whatever gift he has received to serve others, faithfully administering God's grace in its various forms. If anyone speaks, he should do it as one speaking the very words of God. If anyone serves, he should do it with the strength God provides, so that in all things God may be praised through Jesus Christ. To him be the glory and the power for ever and ever. Amen. —1 PETER 4:7–11

For Lorraine Fusco, it may have seemed that her useful days on earth were behind her. Cancer struck at the base of her brain and traveled down her spine, paralyzing her completely. Tubes were used to feed her and help her breathe. The only voluntary movement she could make was to open and shut her eyes and mouth.

There certainly wasn't much Lorraine could do, but she refused to sulk and turn sour, or to bemoan her fate and curse her condition. According to her husband, pastor Bill Fusco, she became a prayer warrior and a shining light of hope. During one stay in the hospital, she so influenced two workers with her joyous outlook that they put their trust in Christ. Later, while her husband served as a college president, she spent entire days praying for each student.

When death finally claimed her, she left a powerful testimony. Lorraine lived joyfully for God despite her trials. She saw her suffering as part of God's will—and she gave every ounce of her energy to serving Him (1 Peter 4:19). She could do nothing but pray and live joyously, but that was enough.

We all have limitations. If we focus on them, we'll find that serving God is a chore. But if we focus on what we can do, we'll make an impact for His kingdom. —DAVE BRANON

God Can Save Anyone!

Therefore I exhort first of all that supplications, prayers, intercessions, and giving of thanks be made for all men, for kings and all who are in authority, that we may lead a quiet and peaceable life in all godliness and reverence. For this is good and acceptable in the sight of God our Savior, who desires all men to be saved and to come to the knowledge of the truth. For there is one God and one Mediator between God and men, the Man Christ Jesus, who gave Himself a ransom for all, to be testified in due time, for which I was appointed a preacher and an apostle—I am speaking the truth in Christ and not lying—a teacher of the Gentiles in faith and truth.

I desire therefore that the men pray everywhere, lifting up holy hands, without wrath and doubting.

—1 Timothy 2:1–8, NKJV

Today, as always, there is an urgent need for us to pray for "all those in authority" (1 Timothy 2:2). But does the word *all* include the most wicked of leaders? Are there ever people in positions of power and influence who are beyond the help of prayer?

The answer to this question can be found by noting the word *therefore* in verse 1, which calls our attention to the immediate context. In 1 Timothy 1:12–17, Paul admitted that he was once a blasphemer, a persecutor, and a violent man (v. 13). He vigorously affirmed that Christ Jesus came into the world to save sinners. Then he added this significant phrase: "of whom I am chief" (v. 15).

Paul explained that he received God's mercy so that Christ would display His limitless grace in him as a pattern for those who are going to believe on Him in the future (v. 16). In effect, Paul was saying, "If I, the worst of sinners, can be saved, anyone can." Paul *therefore* exhorted us to pray for all in authority, because God our Savior desires all to be saved and to embrace His truth (1 Timothy 2:4).

So let's not only pray that honorable leaders will act wisely, but also that ungodly leaders will be saved. Yes, God can save anyone. —JOANIE YODER

Praying with Boldness

O LORD, do not rebuke me in your anger
　　or discipline me in your wrath.
Be merciful to me, LORD, for I am faint;
　　O LORD, heal me, for my bones are in agony.
My soul is in anguish.
　　How long, O LORD, how long?
Turn, O LORD, and deliver me;
　　save me because of your unfailing love . . .
The LORD has heard my cry for mercy;
　　the LORD accepts my prayer.
All my enemies will be ashamed and dismayed;
　　they will turn back in sudden disgrace.

—PSALM 6:1–4, 9–10

*H*ave you ever found it tough to pray? That can happen when we're reluctant to tell God how we're really feeling. We might abruptly stop in mid-sentence, fearful of being disrespectful of our heavenly Father.

A trip through the book of Psalms can help us pray more openly. There we can overhear David's conversations with God and realize that he was not afraid to be completely open and honest with the Lord. David cried out: "O LORD, do not rebuke me in your anger" (Psalm 6:1). "Be merciful to me, LORD, for I am faint" (6:2). "Why, O LORD, do you stand far off?" (10:1). "Do not turn a deaf ear to me" (28:1). "Plead my cause, O LORD" (35:1 NKJV). "Hear my prayer, O God" (54:2). "My thoughts trouble me and I am distraught" (55:2).

Think about David's approach. He was saying to God: "Help me!" "Listen to me!" "Don't be mad at me!" "Where are You?" David boldly went to God and told Him what was on his mind. Yes, God expects us to come to Him with a clean heart, and we need to approach Him with reverence—but we don't have to be afraid to tell God what we're thinking and feeling.

Next time you talk with your heavenly Father—tell it straight. He'll listen, and He'll understand.

—DAVE BRANON

Worrier or Warrior?

For this reason I kneel before the Father, from whom his whole family in heaven and on earth derives its name. I pray that out of his glorious riches he may strengthen you with power through his Spirit in your inner being, so that Christ may dwell in your hearts through faith. And I pray that you, being rooted and established in love, may have power, together with all the saints, to grasp how wide and long and high and deep is the love of Christ, and to know this love that surpasses knowledge—that you may be filled to the measure of all the fullness of God.

Now to him who is able to do immeasurably more than all we ask or imagine, according to his power that is at work within us, to him be glory in the church and in Christ Jesus throughout all generations, for ever and ever! Amen.

—Ephesians 3:14–21

A missionary wrote a newsletter to thank his supporters for being "prayer warriors." Because of a typing error, though, he called them "prayer *worriers*." For some of us, that might be a good description.

In his book *Growing Your Soul*, Neil Wiseman writes, "Prayer must be more than a kind of restatement of fretting worries or a mulling over of problems. Our petitions must move beyond gloomy desperation, which deals mostly with calamity and despair."

During an anxious time in my life, I became a "prayer worrier." I would beg, "Lord, please keep my neighbor from causing me problems tomorrow." Or, "Father, don't let that ornery person spread gossip about me."

But then the Lord taught me to pray *for* people, rather than *against* them. I began to say, "Lord, bless and encourage my neighbor, and help him to sense Your love." Then I watched to see what God would do. The Lord's amazing answers not only helped others but also helped to cure my own anxiety!

Paul was no "prayer worrier." He prayed for God's people that they might know the strength, love, and fullness of God, who is able to do far more than we can ask or even think (Ephesians 3:14–21). Such confidence made Paul a true "prayer warrior." Are your prayers like that?   —JOANIE YODER

When It's Hard To Pray

In the same way, the Spirit helps us in our weakness. We do not know what we ought to pray for, but the Spirit himself intercedes for us with groans that words cannot express. And he who searches our hearts knows the mind of the Spirit, because the Spirit intercedes for the saints in accordance with God's will.

—ROMANS 8:26–27

The Bible tells us that God knows our every thought and every word on our tongue (Psalm 139:1–4). And when we don't know what to pray for, the Holy Spirit "intercedes for us with groans that words cannot express" (Romans 8:26).

These biblical truths assure us that we can have communication with God even without a word being spoken, because He knows the intentions and desires of our heart. What a comfort when we are perplexed or in deep distress! We don't have to worry if we can't find the words to express our thoughts and feelings. We don't have to feel embarrassed if sometimes our sentences break off half-finished. God knows what we want to say. We don't have to feel guilty if our thoughts wander and we have to struggle to keep our minds focused on the Lord.

And for that matter, we don't have to worry about a proper posture in prayer. If we are elderly or arthritic and can't kneel, that's okay. What God cares about is the posture of our heart.

What a wonderful God! No matter how much you falter and stumble in your praying, He hears you. His heart of infinite love responds to the needs and emotions of your own inarticulate heart. So keep on praying!   —VERNON GROUNDS

Unanswered Prayer

Then Jesus went with his disciples to a place called Gethsemane, and he said to them, "Sit here while I go over there and pray." He took Peter and the two sons of Zebedee along with him, and he began to be sorrowful and troubled. Then he said to them, "My soul is overwhelmed with sorrow to the point of death. Stay here and keep watch with me."

Going a little farther, he fell with his face to the ground and prayed, "My Father, if it is possible, may this cup be taken from me. Yet not as I will, but as you will."

Then he returned to his disciples and found them sleeping. "Could you men not keep watch with me for one hour?" he asked Peter. "Watch and pray so that you will not fall into temptation. The spirit is willing, but the body is weak."

He went away a second time and prayed, "My Father, if it is not possible for this cup to be taken away unless I drink it, may your will be done."

When he came back, he again found them sleeping, because their eyes were heavy. So he left them and went away once more and prayed the third time, saying the same thing.

—MATTHEW 26:36–44

Have you or a friend been afflicted with an illness for which there is no medical cure? Has God denied your repeated requests for healing? Has His refusal to say yes caused you to question His purpose?

An article by Carol Bradley tells us about the wisdom of Craig Satterlee, a seminary professor in Chicago. He has been legally blind since birth, with only 20 percent of normal vision. Does he complain, saying that God has not kept His promise to answer prayer? By no means! He believes wholeheartedly that God has given him something even better.

"I am whole," he testifies, "even though I am legally blind." If introduced as a believer in the power of prayer, he graciously explains, "I don't believe in the power of prayer. I believe in the power and presence of God, so I pray." He adds, "We know that God brings light out of darkness, life out of death, hope out of despair. That's what Scripture teaches us."

Prayer isn't the way to get God to do whatever we want. It's an expression of our trust in His power, wisdom, and grace. No matter what we ask God to do for us, we are to have the attitude of Jesus, who said, "Yet not as I will, but as you will" (Matthew 26:39).   —VERNON GROUNDS

Is It Time To Pray?

Rejoice in the Lord always. I will say it again: Rejoice! Let your gentleness be evident to all. The Lord is near. Do not be anxious about anything, but in everything, by prayer and petition, with thanksgiving, present your requests to God. And the peace of God, which transcends all understanding, will guard your hearts and your minds in Christ Jesus. —PHILIPPIANS 4:4–7

$\mathcal{I}$ heard a woman say that she never prayed more than once for anything. She didn't want to weary God with her repeated requests.

The Lord's teaching on prayer in Luke 11 contradicts this notion. He told a parable about a man who went to his friend's house at midnight and asked for some bread to feed his unexpected visitors. At first the friend refused, for he and his family were in bed. Finally he got up and gave him the bread—not out of friendship but because the caller was so persistent (vv. 5–10).

Jesus used this parable to contrast this reluctant friend with our generous heavenly Father. If an irritated neighbor will give in to his friend's persistence and grant his request, how much more readily will our heavenly Father give us all we need!

It's true that God, in His great wisdom, may sometimes delay His answers to prayer. It's also true that we must pray in harmony with the Scriptures and God's will. But Jesus moved beyond those facts to urge us to persist in prayer. He told us to ask, seek, and knock until the answer comes (v. 9).

So don't worry about wearying God. He will never tire of your persistent prayer!   —JOANIE YODER

Praying and Waiting

Then I said: "O LORD, God of heaven, the great and awesome God, who keeps his covenant of love with those who love him and obey his commands, let your ear be attentive and your eyes open to hear the prayer your servant is praying before you day and night for your servants, the people of Israel. I confess the sins we Israelites, including myself and my father's house, have committed against you. We have acted very wickedly toward you. We have not obeyed the commands, decrees and laws you gave your servant Moses.

"Remember the instruction you gave your servant Moses, saying, 'If you are unfaithful, I will scatter you among the nations, but if you return to me and obey my commands, then even if your exiled people are at the farthest horizon, I will gather them from there and bring them to the place I have chosen as a dwelling for my Name.'

"They are your servants and your people, whom you redeemed by your great strength and your mighty hand. O Lord, let your ear be attentive to the prayer of this your servant and to the prayer of your servants who delight in revering your name. Give your servant success today by granting him favor in the presence of this man."

—NEHEMIAH 1:5–11

Christian couple was deeply distressed because their married son and his family had quit going to church and were giving God no place in their lives. As their friend, I advised them to continue showing love, to pray, and to avoid starting arguments. But at the family's annual Christmas gathering, the father gave his son a lecture in the presence of the other siblings. The son and his family left in anger and broke off all contact with his parents.

It's hard to rely on prayer alone when you want something to happen right now. But that is what Nehemiah did. He was distraught by the news that the Israelites in Jerusalem were in grave danger (Nehemiah 1:3–4). He was a man with great leadership ability and in a favorable position to receive help from the king he served, so he was eager to help his people. But he knew that he could be executed for coming into the presence of a Persian king without being invited. Therefore, though he had asked God to give him the opportunity immediately, he trusted God enough to wait. Four months later, the king opened the door for him to make his request (2:1, 4).

It's not always easy to be patient, but God can be trusted. Wait patiently for Him. —HERB VANDER LUGT

73

Morning, Noon, Night

But I call to God,
   and the LORD saves me.
Evening, morning and noon
   I cry out in distress,
   and he hears my voice.
He ransoms me unharmed
   from the battle waged against me,
   even though many oppose me . . .
Cast your cares on the LORD
   and he will sustain you;
   he will never let the righteous fall.
But you, O God, will bring down the wicked
   into the pit of corruption;
bloodthirsty and deceitful men
   will not live out half their days.
But as for me, I trust in you.

—PSALM 55:16–18, 22–23

In May 2003 a powerful earthquake struck northern Algeria. Television news images showed distraught people searching the rubble for survivors, while others numbly visited hospitals and morgues to see if their loved ones were alive or dead. Families stood together weeping and crying out for help. Their burden of uncertainty and grief could be seen, heard, and felt.

If you've experienced an intense feeling of loss, you'll appreciate the words of David in Psalm 55, penned during a painful time in his life. Oppressed by the wicked, hated by his enemies, and betrayed by a friend, David spoke of the anxiety and anguish that threatened to crush his spirit: "Fear and trembling have beset me; horror has overwhelmed me" (v. 5).

But instead of caving in to fear, David poured out his heart to God: "But I call to God, and the LORD saves me. Evening, morning and noon I cry out in distress, and he hears my voice" (vv. 16–17).

Prayer lifts our eyes from personal tragedy to the compassion of God. It enables us to cast our burdens on the Lord instead of breaking under their weight. When our hearts are filled with pain, it's good to call on God in prayer—morning, noon, and night. —DAVID McCASLAND

Panic Prayers

Do not fret because of evil men
    or be envious of those who do wrong;
for like the grass they will soon wither,
    like green plants they will soon die away.
Trust in the LORD and do good;
    dwell in the land and enjoy safe pasture.
Delight yourself in the LORD
    and he will give you the desires of your heart.
Commit your way to the LORD;
    trust in him and he will do this:
He will make your righteousness shine like the dawn,
    the justice of your cause like the noonday sun.
Be still before the LORD and wait patiently for him;
    do not fret when men succeed in their ways,
    when they carry out their wicked schemes.
Refrain from anger and turn from wrath;
    do not fret—it leads only to evil.   —PSALM 37:1–8

In her book *Beyond Our Selves*, Catherine Marshall wrote about learning to surrender her entire life to God through a "prayer of relinquishment." When she encountered situations she feared, she often panicked and exhibited a demanding spirit in prayer: "God, I must have thus and so." God seemed remote. But when she surrendered the dreaded situation to Him to do with it exactly as He pleased, fear left and peace returned. From that moment on, God began working things out.

In Psalm 37, David talked about both commitment and surrender: "Commit your way to the Lord," he said, "trust in him" (v. 5). Committed believers are those who sincerely follow and serve the Lord, and it's appropriate to urge people to have greater commitment. But committing ourselves to God and trusting Him imply surrendering every area of our lives to His wise control, especially when fear and panic overtake us. The promised result of such wholehearted commitment and trust is that God will do what is best for us.

Instead of trying to quell your fears with panic prayers, surrender yourself to God through a prayer of relinquishment, and see what He will do. —JOANIE YODER

Say "Mercy!"

Rejoice in the Lord always. I will say it again: Rejoice! Let your gentleness be evident to all. The Lord is near. Do not be anxious about anything, but in everything, by prayer and petition, with thanksgiving, present your requests to God. And the peace of God, which transcends all understanding, will guard your hearts and your minds in Christ Jesus.   —PHILIPPIANS 4:4–7

*Y*ou may have played the game when you were a child. You interlace your fingers with someone else's and try to bend the other's hands back until one or the other cries "Mercy!" The winner is the one who gets the other person to surrender.

Sometimes we try to play "Mercy" with God when we pray. We have a request that we desperately want answered in a certain way, so we try to "bend His fingers back" and get Him to give in. When it seems we aren't winning, we try a little harder to convince Him by begging or bargaining. We may even give up grudgingly and say, "Lord, You always win! That's not fair!"

God does want honesty of heart. But occasionally in our honesty a demanding spirit comes out. Deep down we know that prayer is not meant to be a contest with God that we try to win. In our wiser moments, we make our requests known to our Lord, surrender them to Him, rely on His grace, and wait for His answers (Philippians 4:6–7). Author Hannah Whitall Smith said, "Be glad and eager to throw yourself unreservedly into His loving arms, and to hand over the reins of government to Him."

Instead of praying with grudging resignation, "Lord, You always win," surrender to Him. Say "Mercy!" —ANNE CETAS

Five-Finger Prayers

Is any one of you in trouble? He should pray. Is anyone happy? Let him sing songs of praise. Is any one of you sick? He should call the elders of the church to pray over him and anoint him with oil in the name of the Lord. And the prayer offered in faith will make the sick person well; the Lord will raise him up. If he has sinned, he will be forgiven. Therefore confess your sins to each other and pray for each other so that you may be healed. The prayer of a righteous man is powerful and effective. —JAMES 5:13–16

*P*rayer is a conversation with God, not a formula. Yet sometimes we might need to use a "method" to freshen up our prayer time. We can pray the Psalms or other Scriptures (such as The Lord's Prayer) or use the ACTS method (Adoration, Confession, Thanksgiving, and Supplication). I recently came across this "Five-Finger Prayer" to use as a guide when praying for others:

- When you fold your hands, the thumb is nearest you. So begin by praying for those closest to you—your loved ones (Philippians 1:3–5).
- The index finger is the pointer. Pray for those who teach—Bible teachers and preachers, and those who teach children (1 Thessalonians 5:25).
- The next finger is the tallest. It reminds you to pray for those in authority over you—national and local leaders, and your supervisor at work (1 Timothy 2:1–2).
- The fourth finger is usually the weakest. Pray for those who are in trouble or who are suffering (James 5:13–16).
- Then comes your little finger. It reminds you of your smallness in relation to God's greatness. Ask Him to supply your needs (Philippians 4:6, 19).

Whatever method you use, just talk with your Father. He wants to hear what's on your heart.   —ANNE CETAS

Job Opening

Be devoted to one another in brotherly love. Honor one another above yourselves. Never be lacking in zeal, but keep your spiritual fervor, serving the Lord. Be joyful in hope, patient in affliction, faithful in prayer. —ROMANS 12:10–12

When my mother-in-law, Lenore Tuttle, went home to be with Jesus at the age of eighty-five, she left a void not only in our family but also in our church. We were now without one of our most faithful prayer warriors.

At Mother Tuttle's funeral, the presiding pastor showed the congregation her prayer box. It contained dozens of prayer cards on which she had written the names of people she prayed for every day, including one that mentioned the pastor's gall bladder surgery. On top of that prayer box was this verse: "But without faith it is impossible to please Him, for he who comes to God must believe that He is, and that He is a rewarder of those who diligently seek Him" (Hebrews 11:6 NKJV). She was a true prayer warrior who diligently sought the Lord.

Each day, many older saints, who have continued steadfastly in prayer (Romans 12:12), leave this earth through death and move on to heaven. This creates a "job opening" for people who will commit themselves to praying faithfully. Many of these positions remain unfilled. Will you fill one of them?

—DAVE BRANON

Why Do You Ask?

Then Jesus went with his disciples to a place called Gethsemane, and he said to them, "Sit here while I go over there and pray." He took Peter and the two sons of Zebedee along with him, and he began to be sorrowful and troubled. Then he said to them, "My soul is overwhelmed with sorrow to the point of death. Stay here and keep watch with me."

Going a little farther, he fell with his face to the ground and prayed, "My Father, if it is possible, may this cup be taken from me. Yet not as I will, but as you will."

Then he returned to his disciples and found them sleeping. "Could you men not keep watch with me for one hour?" he asked Peter. "Watch and pray so that you will not fall into temptation. The spirit is willing, but the body is weak."

He went away a second time and prayed, "My Father, if it is not possible for this cup to be taken away unless I drink it, may your will be done."

When he came back, he again found them sleeping, because their eyes were heavy. So he left them and went away once more and prayed the third time, saying the same thing.

—MATTHEW 26:36–44

You may have heard the saying, "Our small things are great to God's love; our great things are small to His power." How true! There's nothing in our lives so small that God isn't concerned about it—no need, no desire, no burden, no emotion. Likewise, no problem or crisis is so big that it baffles God's wisdom and power. And because He cares for us, we are invited to tell Him about any and all of our concerns (1 Peter 5:7).

Does that mean we can ask God for anything and expect to receive it? For example, does a Christian on a sports team have the right to ask God for victory in a particular game and then expect God to intervene directly to help his team win? And what if players on the other team are also praying for victory?

Faith in our Savior and praying in His name are surely praiseworthy. But let's be sure that what we're asking for is something in line with what we know God would want. It is possible to cross the line from trustful dependence to superstitious selfishness.

Biblical faith is controlled by submission to God's will (1 John 5:14). So every petition must be offered in a way that reflects the attitude of Jesus, who said to His Father, "Not as I will, but as you will" (Matthew 26:39). —VERNON GROUNDS

Who Is Jabez?

Jabez was more honorable than his brothers. His mother had named him Jabez, saying, "I gave birth to him in pain." Jabez cried out to the God of Israel, "Oh, that you would bless me and enlarge my territory! Let your hand be with me, and keep me from harm so that I will be free from pain." And God granted his request. —1 CHRONICLES 4:9–10

Chinese New Year celebrations are fun for children. When relatives and friends get together, it's the custom for adults to give children small red envelopes containing token sums of money. Children often rip open their packets just to get the money, and their parents have to remind them that the giver is more important than the gift.

Similarly, when we study the prayer of Jabez in 1 Chronicles 4:9–10, it is important to remember that the Giver, the Lord, is more important than the gift. If we focus solely on the request of Jabez, it could be easy to make the mistake of turning it into a formula for obtaining what we want from God.

We don't know much about Jabez, except that his mother gave him a name that sounds like the Hebrew word for "distress" or "pain." We're also told that when he grew up, "Jabez was more honorable than his brothers."

What made Jabez "more honorable"? On the basis of his prayer, we can assume that he took his relationship with God seriously. There was no magic in the words of his prayer. Rather, he knew that God is the giver of all things. Jabez was honorable, I believe, because he honored the Lord.

Our prayer today should be to emulate the character of Jabez, who lived to please God. —ALBERT LEE

Surprise Answer

This is how we know what love is: Jesus Christ laid down his life for us. And we ought to lay down our lives for our brothers. If anyone has material possessions and sees his brother in need but has no pity on him, how can the love of God be in him? Dear children, let us not love with words or tongue but with actions and in truth. This then is how we know that we belong to the truth, and how we set our hearts at rest in his presence whenever our hearts condemn us. For God is greater than our hearts, and he knows everything.

Dear friends, if our hearts do not condemn us, we have confidence before God and receive from him anything we ask, because we obey his commands and do what pleases him. And this is his command: to believe in the name of his Son, Jesus Christ, and to love one another as he commanded us. —1 JOHN 3:16–23

While Josh McDowell was attending seminary in California, his father went home to be with the Lord. His mother had died years earlier, but Josh was not sure of her salvation. He became depressed, thinking that she might be lost. The thought obsessed him. "Lord," he prayed, "somehow give me the answer so I can get back to normal. I've just got to know." It seemed like an impossible request.

Two days later, Josh drove out to the ocean and walked to the end of a pier to be alone. There sat an old woman in a lawn chair, fishing. "Where's your home originally?" she asked.

"Michigan—Union City," Josh replied. "Nobody's heard of it. I tell people it's a suburb of—"

"Battle Creek," interrupted the woman. "I had a cousin from there. Did you know the McDowell family?"

Stunned, Josh responded, "Yes, I'm Josh McDowell."

"I can't believe it," said the woman. "I'm a cousin to your mother."

"Do you remember anything at all about my mother's spiritual life?" asked Josh.

"Why sure—your mom and I were just girls when a tent revival came to town. It was the fourth night—we both went forward to accept Christ."

"Praise God!" shouted Josh.

If we are obedient to God, He delights to give us what we ask when it is in His will. Let's never underestimate God's desire to respond to our prayers. A surprise answer may be just around the corner.

—DENNIS DE HAAN

Letting Jesus In

"To the angel of the church in Laodicea write: These are the words of the Amen, the faithful and true witness, the ruler of God's creation.

"I know your deeds, that you are neither cold nor hot. I wish you were either one or the other! So, because you are lukewarm—neither hot nor cold—I am about to spit you out of my mouth. You say, 'I am rich; I have acquired wealth and do not need a thing.' But you do not realize that you are wretched, pitiful, poor, blind and naked. I counsel you to buy from me gold refined in the fire, so you can become rich; and white clothes to wear, so you can cover your shameful nakedness; and salve to put on your eyes, so you can see.

"Those whom I love I rebuke and discipline. So be earnest, and repent. Here I am! I stand at the door and knock. If anyone hears my voice and opens the door, I will come in and eat with him, and he with me. To him who overcomes, I will give the right to sit with me on my throne, just as I overcame and sat down with my Father on his throne. He who has an ear, let him hear what the Spirit says to the churches." —REVELATION 3:14–22

How we complicate prayer! We think its effectiveness depends solely on the strength of our faith, the fervency of our emotions, or the clarity with which we articulate our needs. But it is far more simple—and profound—than that.

The Norwegian theologian Ole Hallesby gives one of the best definitions of prayer I have ever read. He says, "To pray is nothing more involved than to let Jesus into our needs. To pray is to give Jesus permission to employ His powers in the alleviation of our distress."

These words underscore the one spiritual condition God looks for in the hearts of His children: helplessness. He wants us to acknowledge that we're short on wisdom, strength, and the ability to know and do the right, even when we have everything in control. Any utterance, even yearning, that springs from this attitude and is directed toward God is prayer in its purest form. Whether clothed in words or groanings, it ascends to His throne and is heard by our sympathetic High Priest.

The greatest hindrance to prayer, then, is that we do not consciously maintain a humble dependence upon the Lord. Like the Laodicean Christians, we think that we "do not need a thing," and we do not know that we are "wretched, pitiful, poor, blind, and naked." But when our prayer is based on helplessness--whether we need restoration, victory, guidance, knowledge, or strength--it always opens the door and lets Jesus in.

—DENNIS DE HAAN

Prayer with Thanksgiving

Do not be anxious about anything, but in everything, by prayer and petition, with thanksgiving, present your requests to God. And the peace of God, which transcends all understanding, will guard your hearts and your minds in Christ Jesus.

Finally, brothers, whatever is true, whatever is noble, whatever is right, whatever is pure, whatever is lovely, whatever is admirable—if anything is excellent or praiseworthy—think about such things. Whatever you have learned or received or heard from me, or seen in me—put it into practice. And the God of peace will be with you.

I rejoice greatly in the Lord that at last you have renewed your concern for me. Indeed, you have been concerned, but you had no opportunity to show it. I am not saying this because I am in need, for I have learned to be content whatever the circumstances. I know what it is to be in need, and I know what it is to have plenty. I have learned the secret of being content in any and every situation, whether well fed or hungry, whether living in plenty or in want. I can do everything through him who gives me strength.

—PHILIPPIANS 4:6–13

*J*udy's rare brain condition required delicate surgery. The risky procedure took place in the operating theater at a research hospital with many doctors and medical students observing.

Just before the operation was to begin, the surgeon asked, "Do you have any questions?" Judy replied, "May I pray for you?" With many looking on, she thanked God for the surgeon's great skill, asked wisdom for him, and committed the surgery into the Lord's hands.

How it must delight God's heart when we unashamedly bring our cares to Him with thanksgiving! Judy didn't ask God to spare her life. She was sure that her heavenly Father knew how much she longed to live. She simply thanked Him for the surgeon's knowledge and skill and entrusted herself to the Great Physician's special care.

Judy got a new lease on life that day. And those doctors got a firsthand look at faith in the true and living God. Paul said, "In everything, by prayer and petition, with thanksgiving, present your requests to God" (Philippians 4:6). Notice that God does not promise to give you all you want, but rather, "the peace of God, which transcends all understanding, will guard your hearts and minds in Christ Jesus" (v. 7). What a gift!

—Dennis De Haan

More Than Wishing

And when you pray, do not keep on babbling like pagans, for they think they will be heard because of their many words. Do not be like them, for your Father knows what you need before you ask him.

"This, then, is how you should pray:

"'Our Father in heaven,
hallowed be your name,
your kingdom come,
your will be done
on earth as it is in heaven.
Give us today our daily bread.
Forgive us our debts,
as we also have forgiven our debtors.
And lead us not into temptation,
but deliver us from the evil one.'"

—MATTHEW 6:7–13

As a child, C. S. Lewis enjoyed reading the books of E. Nesbit, especially *Five Children and It*. In this book, brothers and sisters on a summer holiday discover an ancient sand fairy who grants them one wish each day. But every wish brings the children more trouble than happiness because they can't foresee the results of getting everything they ask for.

The Bible tells us to make our requests known to God (Philippians 4:6). But prayer is much more than telling God what we want Him to do for us. When Jesus taught His disciples how to pray, He began by reminding them, "Your Father knows what you need before you ask him" (Matthew 6:8).

What we call "The Lord's Prayer" is more about living in a growing, trusting relationship with our heavenly Father than about getting what we want from Him. As we grow in faith, our prayers will become less of a wish list and more of an intimate conversation with the Lord.

Toward the end of his life, C. S. Lewis wrote, "If God had granted all the silly prayers I've made in my life, where should I be now?"

Prayer is placing ourselves in the presence of God to receive from Him what we really need. —David McCasland

Sleepless Nights

Keep me safe, O God,
  for in you I take refuge.
I said to the LORD, "You are my Lord;
  apart from you I have no good thing." . . .
LORD, you have assigned me my portion and my cup;
  you have made my lot secure.
The boundary lines have fallen for me in pleasant places;
  surely I have a delightful inheritance.
I will praise the LORD, who counsels me;
  even at night my heart instructs me.
I have set the LORD always before me.
  Because he is at my right hand,
  I will not be shaken.
Therefore my heart is glad and my tongue rejoices;
  my body also will rest secure,
because you will not abandon me to the grave,
  nor will you let your Holy One see decay.
You have made known to me the path of life;
  you will fill me with joy in your presence,
  with eternal pleasures at your right hand.

—PSALM 16:1–2, 6–11

The psalmist David had his dark, lonely nights when everything seemed out of control. Doubts and fears assailed him, and there was no escape from his problems. He tossed and turned just as we do, but then he turned to his Shepherd (Psalm 23:1) and reminded himself of the Lord's presence. That brought peace to his anxious, troubled soul. David said, "Because he is at my right hand, I shall not be shaken" (16:8).

We too have occasions of wakefulness when anxious thoughts jostle one another for attention, when we curse the darkness, and when we long for sleep. But we mustn't fret, for darkness can be our friend. God is present in it, visiting us, counseling us, instructing us in the night. Perhaps on our beds, as nowhere else, we may hear God's voice. We can listen to His thoughts and meditate on His Word.

We can talk to the Lord about every concern, casting our care on Him (1 Peter 5:7). We can talk about our failures, our conflicts, our challenges, our anxieties, and our frustrations— all the things that stress us out and render us sleepless—and listen to what He has to say. That's what can set us apart from ordinary insomniacs. That's the secret of quiet rest.

—DAVID ROPER

You May Get What You Pray For

When our fathers were in Egypt,
    they gave no thought to your miracles;
they did not remember your many kindnesses,
    and they rebelled by the sea, the Red Sea.
Yet he saved them for his name's sake,
    to make his mighty power known.
He rebuked the Red Sea, and it dried up;
    he led them through the depths as through a desert.
He saved them from the hand of the foe;
    from the hand of the enemy he redeemed them . . .
But they soon forgot what he had done
    and did not wait for his counsel.
In the desert they gave in to their craving;
    in the wasteland they put God to the test.
So he gave them what they asked for,
    but sent a wasting disease upon them.

—PSALM 106:7–10, 13–15

*I*t's possible to have a fat wallet and a skinny soul. We see this confirmed in Psalm 106, which is a poetic description of the Israelites' inward poverty despite their outward wealth.

The psalmist recalled how God in His grace had repeatedly rescued His people as they traveled through the desert (106:7-11). He supplied them each day with manna (Exodus 16:4-16), but the people didn't like the diet. Instead, they fondly recalled the menu they were served as slaves in Egypt and grumbled, "If only we had meat to eat! . . . We never see anything but this manna!" (Numbers 11:4, 6).

God got tired of all their griping, and He judged them in an interesting way—He gave them what they asked for. A wind blowing in from the sea covered the ground with quail. For two days and a night the greedy people feasted on quail, but while the flesh was still between their teeth God hit them with a deadly plague (Numbers 11:31-34). The psalmist commented, "He gave them their request, but sent leanness into their soul" (106:15 NKJV).

Our rebellious desires do not become good prayers just because we address them to God. How much better to say, "Above all, Lord, I want Your will!" That way, we'll not only get what we pray for, we'll want what we get.

—HADDON ROBINSON

Our God-Listener

O you who hear prayer,
  to you all men will come.
When we were overwhelmed by sins,
  you forgave our transgressions.
Blessed are those you choose
  and bring near to live in your courts!
We are filled with the good things of your house,
  of your holy temple.
You answer us with awesome deeds of righteousness,
  O God our Savior,
the hope of all the ends of the earth
  and of the farthest seas,
who formed the mountains by your power,
  having armed yourself with strength,
who stilled the roaring of the seas,
  the roaring of their waves,
  and the turmoil of the nations.
Those living far away fear your wonders;
  where morning dawns and evening fades
  you call forth songs of joy.   —PSALM 65:2–8

*E*very time a Christian prays, he is exercising a God-given privilege. It enables him to have immediate and continuous access to the One who is omnipotent, who listens in heaven, and who can and does change the affairs of men. By contrast, the thoughts and needs of some secular men are also being directed into the heavens, but not to the God of the Bible.

One group of scientists claims to have calculated mathematically that as many as fifty million civilizations may exist somewhere out in space. They believe that some of them may have found the methods to improve our lives and control the time of our death. In November 1974, this speculation was acted upon. By means of technology these scientists beamed a message to a cluster of stars on the outer edge of our galaxy. But even if that signal were picked up, it would take an estimated 48,000 years before an answer came back.

To Christians, these efforts are a waste of time, for they appear destined to ultimate failure. Even more unfortunate, however, is the fact that we who do have an effective contact with "another world" fail to take it more seriously. Every child of God has within him the capacity to get in touch, not with other creatures, but with the Creator! We have instant, continual access through prayer to the One who stretched out all the galaxies in the heavens and who promises to hear us and answer according to His will.

In light of our relationship to Him, let's pray with renewed confidence as those who know and appreciate our God-listener.

—MART DE HAAN

Persistent Praying

Then Jesus told his disciples a parable to show them that they should always pray and not give up. He said: "In a certain town there was a judge who neither feared God nor cared about men. And there was a widow in that town who kept coming to him with the plea, 'Grant me justice against my adversary.'

"For some time he refused. But finally he said to himself, 'Even though I don't fear God or care about men, yet because this widow keeps bothering me, I will see that she gets justice, so that she won't eventually wear me out with her coming!' "

And the Lord said, "Listen to what the unjust judge says. And will not God bring about justice for his chosen ones, who cry out to him day and night? Will he keep putting them off? I tell you, he will see that they get justice, and quickly. However, when the Son of Man comes, will he find faith on the earth?"

—LUKE 18:1–8

The Associated Press carried an interesting story about a group of post office customers who succeeded in speeding up some slow-moving service. According to those who were there, the lines "were moving slower than paint dries." One man said, "It was like watching grass grow." There were twenty-six patrons jammed into two lines. They realized they weren't getting enough attention, so one man organized the group. In an uncommon show of unity, the twenty-six shouted together, "We want service!" Two minutes later, another clerk ambled out and without cracking a smile said, "Next?" Well, the twenty-six knew they were on to something, so they tried it again. You guessed it, one more clerk appeared. An amused customer summed up the situation like this: "I got through that line in four minutes. I've never seen anything like it!"

In some ways this is a modern version of Christ's parable of the unjust judge in which He taught a vital truth about prayer. Now, Jesus wasn't saying that it's necessary to demand things from God. Rather, He wanted us to see the importance of perseverance. To make His point, He set up a contrast. He said that if men can be persuaded by persistent asking, how much more will our gracious Heavenly Father give ear to our pleadings!

The Lord loves us and longs to meet our needs. He's waiting to hear our petitions, and we can be confident that He will respond in His own way and in His own time. God teaches us to be persistent in our praying!   —MART DE HAAN

We've Got It Covered

In the morning, O LORD, you hear my voice;
in the morning I lay my requests before you
and wait in expectation . . .
Lead me, O LORD, in your righteousness
because of my enemies—
make straight your way before me . . .
But let all who take refuge in you be glad;
let them ever sing for joy.
Spread your protection over them,
that those who love your name may rejoice in you.
For surely, O LORD, you bless the righteous;
you surround them with your favor as with a shield.

—PSALM 5:3, 8, 11 –12

*B*efore we go to the grocery store, we make out a shopping list. Before we accept a responsibility, we check to see what it involves. Likewise, when we plunge into a new day, we should prepare for it. As we think about what lies ahead, we can commit it all to the Lord. Then we'll be able to take advantage of the day's opportunities and to cope with its disappointments.

Ray Ortlund, in *The Best Half of Life*, wrote:

> I like to start out the morning covering the whole day by prayer. After a time of praise and confession, I take out my appointment book and pray through the hours. I pray for everyone I am scheduled to see. I ask that I might be helpful to them, but also open to what they may have for me. I pray for the unscheduled ones I will bump into. I've found that if I pray over my interruptions and get them squarely under God's sovereign control, they don't irritate me. I realize they are part of God's plan. So, pray over your day. Pray about every phone conversation; pray about your lunchtime. . . Pray over evening; pray and think about the time you'll be with those you love the most. Pray through the day before you experience it. Then relax. Whatever comes—you've got it covered.

Each day presents trying circumstances, challenges, and opportunities. So before we begin our activities, let's turn the day over to God. Then, whatever happens, we've got it covered!

—DAVE EGNER

Help by Praying

We do not want you to be uninformed, brothers, about the hardships we suffered in the province of Asia. We were under great pressure, far beyond our ability to endure, so that we despaired even of life. Indeed, in our hearts we felt the sentence of death. But this happened that we might not rely on ourselves but on God, who raises the dead. He has delivered us from such a deadly peril, and he will deliver us. On him we have set our hope that he will continue to deliver us, as you help us by your prayers. Then many will give thanks on our behalf for the gracious favor granted us in answer to the prayers of many.

—2 CORINTHIANS 1:8–11

*S*ome Christians feel frustrated because they are not able to serve the Lord as actively as they would like. They may be limited by some physical disease. Or perhaps family or work responsibilities are keeping them from doing more for Christ. They want to help in the Lord's work, but they are restricted.

Any believer, though, can serve the Lord through prayer. Paul spoke about the hardships he suffered in Asia Minor and how the prayers of others helped him. He was under tremendous pressure, but God gave him strength and delivered him. The Christians in Corinth were actively involved in Paul's ministry, for he wrote to them, "You help us by your prayers."

We tend to view prayer as only indirect involvement in ministry, but it may be the most important thing we can do. God's specially called servants need the faithful prayer support of His people. Whatever their task—pastoring, administering, or teaching—they may be facing tremendous pressure. They may be under attack by the enemy. They may be struggling against physical affliction or making far-reaching decisions. Whatever it is, they cannot do it alone. And we can be helping them. How? By praying.

Let us never think we can't be active in the Lord's work. We can by "helping together in prayer."   —DAVE EGNER

Have You Prayed?

Rejoice in the Lord always. I will say it again: Rejoice! Let your gentleness be evident to all. The Lord is near. Do not be anxious about anything, but in everything, by prayer and petition, with thanksgiving, present your requests to God. And the peace of God, which transcends all understanding, will guard your hearts and your minds in Christ Jesus . . .

I rejoice greatly in the Lord that at last you have renewed your concern for me. Indeed, you have been concerned, but you had no opportunity to show it. I am not saying this because I am in need, for I have learned to be content whatever the circumstances. I know what it is to be in need, and I know what it is to have plenty. I have learned the secret of being content in any and every situation, whether well fed or hungry, whether living in plenty or in want. I can do everything through him who gives me strength. —PHILIPPIANS 4:4–7, 10–13

Several years ago I moved to England, but I have traveled back to the United States many times since, often staying with the same families. One family lived in a farmhouse where a tiny upstairs room always awaited me.

I will never forget one visit when, as usual, I lugged my suitcase up the familiar stairs. This time, however, a secret burden on my heart felt heavier than my luggage. As I neared the top of the steps, I saw an old plaque that I had noticed on previous visits. It read: *Have You Prayed About It?*

Panting physically and spiritually, I had to admit, "No, I haven't!" So I slipped to my knees and finally talked to God about the problem.

Instead of being anxious for nothing, I had become anxious about everything. Instead of praying about everything, I had prayed about nothing. But now, through prayer, my heavy load of worry became God's, and His lightweight gift of peace became mine.

In his book *Tyranny of the Urgent,* Charles Hummel writes that if we are prayerless, "we are saying, with our actions if not our lips, that we do not need God." The deciding factor on how we carry our burdens lies in our answer to the question on that old-fashioned plaque: Have you prayed about it?

—JOANIE YODER

Spiritual Jotting

Oh, how I love your law!
*   I meditate on it all day long.*
Your commands make me wiser than my enemies,
*   for they are ever with me.*
I have more insight than all my teachers,
*   for I meditate on your statutes.*
I have more understanding than the elders,
*   for I obey your precepts.*
I have kept my feet from every evil path
*   so that I might obey your word.*
I have not departed from your laws,
*   for you yourself have taught me.*
How sweet are your words to my taste,
*   sweeter than honey to my mouth!*
I gain understanding from your precepts;
*   therefore I hate every wrong path.*

—PSALM 119:97–104

I have met many young mothers who are discouraged by their inadequate devotional life. The term "quiet time" only reminds them how little "quiet" or "time" they have for Bible reading, prayer, and meditation.

When my children were young, I was inspired by a speaker (also a mother) who shared how she overcame this dilemma during her child-rearing years. Throughout her house she placed pencils and notepads on high surfaces, well above the reach of her toddlers. During the day, wherever she was, she would jot down insights, prayer needs, or Bible verses as they came to mind. Each evening she would gather up her jottings—the ingredients of a spiritual feast she had been preparing all day. How eagerly she welcomed the opportunity to nourish her hungry spirit with her Bible and her jottings! As I began putting her method to the test, my daily devotions became what they needed to be—a workable vehicle for strengthening my devotion to Christ.

Whether you're an overworked mother, or simply overworked, I recommend "spiritual jotting," both now and as a lifelong habit. Not only will it put more devotion into your devotions, it will also bring you closer to fulfilling Paul's admonition to "pray without ceasing" (1 Thessalonians 5:17 NKJV).

—JOANIE YODER

Prayer Malfunction

Dear friends, if our hearts do not condemn us, we have confidence before God and receive from him anything we ask, because we obey his commands and do what pleases him. And this is his command: to believe in the name of his Son, Jesus Christ, and to love one another as he commanded us. Those who obey his commands live in him, and he in them. And this is how we know that he lives in us: We know it by the Spirit he gave us.

—I JOHN 3:21–24

In a box of my father's old tools I found a hand drill that was at least sixty years old. I could barely get the wheel to turn. The gears were clogged with dirt, and the pieces that hold the drill bit in place were missing. But I wanted to see if I could get it to work.

I began by wiping the accumulated dirt and sawdust off the gears. Then I oiled them. At first they turned hard and slow, but I kept working them. Soon the gears were turning smoothly. Then I saw a cap at the top of the handle. Unscrewing it, I discovered the missing parts that would hold the bit in place. I placed them in the drill, inserted a bit, and easily bored a neat hole in a piece of wood.

Working with that old drill taught me something about prayer. Jesus said we will receive from God what we ask of Him (Matthew 7:7–8). But there are conditions. For example, John said we must obey God and do what pleases Him (1 John 3:22). This includes believing in His Son and loving one another (v. 23). If we don't meet God's conditions, our prayers will be ineffective—just like that old drill.

If your prayer-life is malfunctioning, make sure you're meeting the conditions. When you do, you can be confident that your prayers will be effective.　　　—DAVE EGNER

The Only One

I sought the LORD, and he answered me;
he delivered me from all my fears.
Those who look to him are radiant;
their faces are never covered with shame.
This poor man called, and the LORD heard him;
he saved him out of all his troubles . . .
The eyes of the LORD are on the righteous
and his ears are attentive to their cry; . . .

The righteous cry out, and the LORD hears them;
he delivers them from all their troubles.

—PSALM 34:4–6, 15, 17

As a teacher with many years of experience in high school and college classrooms, I have observed many kinds of students. One in particular is what I call the "just me and the teacher" student. This pupil has a kind of one-on-one conversation with the teacher—almost as if no one else were in the class. The teacher's rhetorical questions, for instance, result in verbal answers from this student—oblivious to anyone else's reaction. While the class is filled with other pupils, this one seems to think it's "just me and the teacher."

As I watched one of these students recently and saw him command the teacher's attention, I thought: He's on to something. He has the focus we all need to have when we pray.

The thought that millions of other Christians are talking to God as we pray should never cause us to feel that we are less important. No, as we talk to our everywhere-present, all-knowing, all-powerful God, we can be confident that He is giving us His full attention. David said, "This poor man called, and the LORD heard him" (Psalm 34:6).

God directs single-minded attention toward your praise, your requests, and your concerns. When you pray, to Him you are the only one. —DAVE BRANON

Keep on Praying

"Now then, stand still and see this great thing the LORD is about to do before your eyes! Is it not wheat harvest now? I will call upon the LORD to send thunder and rain. And you will realize what an evil thing you did in the eyes of the LORD when you asked for a king."

Then Samuel called upon the LORD, and that same day the LORD sent thunder and rain. So all the people stood in awe of the LORD and of Samuel.

The people all said to Samuel, "Pray to the LORD your God for your servants so that we will not die, for we have added to all our other sins the evil of asking for a king."

"Do not be afraid," Samuel replied. "You have done all this evil; yet do not turn away from the LORD, but serve the LORD with all your heart. Do not turn away after useless idols. They can do you no good, nor can they rescue you, because they are useless. For the sake of his great name the LORD will not reject his people, because the LORD was pleased to make you his own. As for me, far be it from me that I should sin against the LORD by failing to pray for you. And I will teach you the way that is good and right. But be sure to fear the LORD and serve him faithfully with all your heart; consider what great things he has done for you. Yet if you persist in doing evil, both you and your king will be swept away."   —I SAMUEL 12:16–25

A godly mother told about her two sons now in their forties. Although raised in a Christian home, they turned their backs on the Lord. Neither could hold a job. One was in jail; the other had recently been released. Tears fell from this mother's eyes as she told of their terrible language and disregard for the laws of God and man. But then she said, "I still pray for them both every day. I plead with the Lord not to give up on them—to bring them back to Himself. I'm not giving up. I'll pray for them until the Lord calls me home."

In 1 Samuel 12, we read a story that's both terrible and marvelous. Israel had been rebellious. The people had sinned against the Lord throughout the period of the judges, and now they compounded their disregard for the Lord by demanding a king. To show them their wickedness, Samuel asked the Lord to send thunder and hail on the wheat harvest (vv. 16–18). When the Lord answered, the people were terrified. But then Samuel spoke to them with reassurance. In spite of their rebellion, he promised to keep on praying for them as they began living under Saul, their new king.

How many times have we wanted to give up praying for someone? How often have we thought that it would do no good, that we were wasting our time? Samuel may have felt that way with Israel, but he didn't give in to his frustration and disappointment. Let's follow his example. Keep on praying!

—DAVE EGNER

Window Shopping

Then they came to Jericho. As Jesus and his disciples, together with a large crowd, were leaving the city, a blind man, Bartimaeus (that is, the Son of Timaeus), was sitting by the roadside begging. When he heard that it was Jesus of Nazareth, he began to shout, "Jesus, Son of David, have mercy on me!"

Many rebuked him and told him to be quiet, but he shouted all the more, "Son of David, have mercy on me!"

Jesus stopped and said, "Call him." So they called to the blind man, "Cheer up! On your feet! He's calling you." Throwing his cloak aside, he jumped to his feet and came to Jesus.

"What do you want me to do for you?" Jesus asked him. The blind man said, "Rabbi, I want to see."

"Go," said Jesus, "your faith has healed you." Immediately he received his sight and followed Jesus along the road.

—MARK 10:46–52

The Lord encourages us to come to Him with our needs (Matthew 7:7–12), and we should be specific. Our prayers should not be vague generalities such as "save the world," but pointed—"save my spouse, my friend, my neighbor, my co-worker."

Catherine Marshall compared generalized, non-focused prayers to window-shopping. She wrote, "Window-shopping can be enjoyable—but there it ends. It costs nothing. We are just looking, have no intention of buying anything; so we bring nothing home to show for the hours of browsing. Too many of our prayers—private and public—are just browsing among possible petitions, not down to cases at all."

We can learn from Bartimaeus. He knew that the Lord had the ability to grant his request. He knew exactly what he wanted. When the Lord turned to this blind man and gave him an opportunity to make a request, Bartimaeus said without hesitation, "I want to be able to see." He believed that Jesus could heal him. Bartimaeus asked—and received. His plea was specific.

May we too have the faith and courage to ask the Lord for our specific needs and trust Him to do what is best for us. Then we'll avoid the ineffectiveness of window-shopping prayer.

—DAVE EGNER

Grass on Your Path?

The administrators and the satraps tried to find grounds for charges against Daniel in his conduct of government affairs, but they were unable to do so. They could find no corruption in him, because he was trustworthy and neither corrupt nor negligent. Finally these men said, "We will never find any basis for charges against this man Daniel unless it has something to do with the law of his God."

So the administrators and the satraps went as a group to the king and said: "O King Darius, live forever! The royal administrators, prefects, satraps, advisers and governors have all agreed that the king should issue an edict and enforce the decree that anyone who prays to any god or man during the next thirty days, except to you, O king, shall be thrown into the lions' den. Now, O king, issue the decree and put it in writing so that it cannot be altered—in accordance with the laws of the Medes and Persians, which cannot be repealed." So King Darius put the decree in writing.

Now when Daniel learned that the decree had been published, he went home to his upstairs room where the windows opened toward Jerusalem. Three times a day he got down on his knees and prayed, giving thanks to his God, just as he had done before.

—Daniel 6:4–10

In one region of Africa, the first converts to Christianity were diligent about praying. In fact, the believers each had their own special place outside the village where they went to pray in solitude. The villagers reached these "prayer rooms" by using their own private footpaths through the brush. When grass began to grow over one of these trails, it was evident that the person to whom it belonged was not praying very much.

Because these new Christians were concerned for each other's spiritual welfare, a unique custom sprang up. Whenever anyone noticed an overgrown "prayer path," he or she would go to the person and lovingly warn, "Friend, there's grass on your path!"

In today's Scripture we read that three times a day Daniel "got down on his knees and prayed, giving thanks to his God" (Daniel 6:10). We too must maintain a regular schedule of meeting the Lord in prayer. It would be well for each of us to check and see if there has been any tendency to neglect our times with God.

Have you met with the Lord yet today? Do you regularly come to "the throne of grace" to "obtain mercy and find grace to help in time of need"? (Hebrews 4:16 NKJV). Is there any "grass on your path"?   —RICHARD DE HAAN

Selfish Prayers

What causes fights and quarrels among you? Don't they come from your desires that battle within you? You want something but don't get it. You kill and covet, but you cannot have what you want. You quarrel and fight. You do not have, because you do not ask God. When you ask, you do not receive, because you ask with wrong motives, that you may spend what you get on your pleasures.

You adulterous people, don't you know that friendship with the world is hatred toward God? Anyone who chooses to be a friend of the world becomes an enemy of God. Or do you think Scripture says without reason that the spirit he caused to live in us envies intensely? But he gives us more grace. That is why Scripture says:

"God opposes the proud
but gives grace to the humble."

Submit yourselves, then, to God. Resist the devil, and he will flee from you. Come near to God and he will come near to you. Wash your hands, you sinners, and purify your hearts, you double-minded. Grieve, mourn and wail. Change your laughter to mourning and your joy to gloom. Humble yourselves before the Lord, and he will lift you up. —JAMES 4:1–10

*S*ome people see God as a supernatural change-agent who answers their every whim, a kind of divine genie who stands before them to grant their every wish.

Take the well-meaning fan at a basketball game who said, "Our team's behind. Pray!" Or the executive who left thirty minutes late for an important sales presentation and asked her colleagues to pray that she would get there on time.

People who are preoccupied with such self-centered requests have a very shallow view of God and His redemptive purpose in the world. They see Him as One who exists to provide for their wants and needs, alleviate all their suffering, and make their lives as pleasant as possible. They may get that kind of picture of God from secular novels but not from the Bible.

All attempts to manipulate a sovereign God into serving our own selfish purposes insult Him. And James related selfish praying to "friendship with the world," which he said is "hatred toward God" (James 4:3–4).

For the next few days, analyze your prayers. If they are usually for your own convenience, comfort, or pleasure, it's time to change your praying. —DAVE EGNER

About the Authors

Henry Bosch served as the first editor of the daily devotional booklet that became *Our Daily Bread* (ODB) and contributed many of the earliest articles. He was also one of the singers on the Radio Bible Class live broadcast.

Dave Branon has done freelance writing for many years and has published more than thirteen books. Dave taught English and coached basketball and baseball at the high school level before coming to RBC Ministries (RBC), where he is now the Managing Editor of *Sports Spectrum* magazine.

Anne Cetas is Assistant Managing Editor on the editorial staff at RBC Ministries and has been with the ministry for twenty-five years. Anne and her husband Carl also work as mentors in an inner-city ministry. "It's the most challenging ministry I've ever loved," says Anne. She also teaches Sunday school and disciples new believers.

Dennis De Haan is a nephew of RBC founder Dr. M. R. De Haan. He pastored two churches in Iowa and Michigan before joining the RBC staff in 1971. He served as Associate Editor of ODB from 1973 until 1982, and then as Editor until June 1995. Now retired, Dennis continues editing for ODB on a part-time basis.

Mart De Haan is the grandson of RBC founder, Dr. M. R. De Haan, and the son of former president Richard W. De Haan. Having served at RBC for over thirty years, Mart is heard regularly on the *Discover the Word* radio program and seen on *Day of Discovery* television. Mart is also a contributing writer for ODB, the Discovery Series Bible study booklets, and a monthly column on timely issues called "Been Thinking About."

Richard De Haan was President of RBC Ministries and teacher on RBC programs for twenty years. He was the son of RBC founder Dr. M. R. De Haan and wrote a number of full-length books and study booklets for RBC. Often called "the encourager," Richard was committed to faithfulness to God's Word and to integrity as a ministry. His favorite expression was "Trust in God and do the right." Richard went to be with the Lord in 2002.

Dave Egner is now retired from RBC. He was (until June 2002) Managing Editor of *Campus Journal*. He has written Discovery Series study booklets and articles for a variety of publications. Dave taught English and writing for ten years at Grand Rapids Baptist College (now Cornerstone University) before coming to RBC.

Vernon Grounds, Chancellor of Denver Seminary, has had an extensive preaching, teaching, and counseling ministry, and was president of Denver Seminary. In addition to writing articles for ODB, he has also written many books and magazine articles

Albert Lee is the Director of International Ministries for RBC and has the passion, vision, and energy to help RBC Ministries spread its work. He grew up in Singapore, attended Singapore Bible College and Taylor University in Indiana, and served with Youth for Christ from 1971-1999.

Julie Ackerman Link is a seasoned writer and editor who has worked on many projects for RBC Ministries and Discovery House Publishers, including the Loving God series. She has been writing for *Our Daily Bread* since December 2000.

David McCasland researches and helps develop biographical documentaries for *Day of Discovery* television, in addition to writing ODB articles His books include the award-winning biography *Oswald Chambers: Abandoned to God,* a compilation of *The Complete Works of Oswald Chambers*, and *Pure Gold,* a biography of Eric Liddell.

Haddon Robinson is the discussion leader for the RBC Ministries' *Discover the Word* radio program, in addition to writing for *Our Daily Bread.* Dr. Robinson teaches at Gordon-Conwell Theological Seminary where he is the Harold J. Ockenga Distinguished Professor of Preaching. He has authored several books, including *Biblical Preaching* and *Biblical Sermons,* which is currently used as text for preaching in 120 seminaries and Bible colleges throughout the world.

David Roper was a pastor for more than thirty years and now directs Idaho Mountain Ministries, a retreat dedicated to the encouragement of pastoral couples. He enjoys fly-fishing, fly-tying, hiking, and just being streamside in the mountains with his wife Carolyn. He is the author of eleven books, including *Psalm 23: The Song of a Passionate Heart.*

Herb Vander Lugt is Senior Research Editor for RBC Ministries and has been at RBC since 1966. In addition to ODB articles, he also writes Discovery Series booklets and reviews all study and devotional materials. Herb has pastored six churches, and since retiring from the pastorate in 1989 has held three interim pastor positions.

Joanie Yoder, a favorite among ODB readers, went home to be with her Savior in 2004. She and her husband established a Christian rehabilitation center for drug addicts in England many years ago. Widowed in 1982, she learned to rely on the Lord's help and strength. She wrote with hope about true dependence on God and His life-changing power.